T0284304

Beat Your Writer's Block

SUPER
QUICK
SKILLS

Beat Your Writer's Block

Andrew
Edwards

Los Angeles | London | New Delhi
Singapore | Washington DC | Melbourne

Los Angeles | London | New Delhi
Singapore | Washington DC | Melbourne

SAGE Publications Ltd
1 Oliver's Yard
55 City Road
London EC1Y 1SP

SAGE Publications Inc.
2455 Teller Road
Thousand Oaks, California 91320

SAGE Publications India Pvt Ltd
B 1/I 1 Mohan Cooperative Industrial Area
Mathura Road
New Delhi 110 044

SAGE Publications Asia-Pacific Pte Ltd
3 Church Street
#10-04 Samsung Hub
Singapore 049483

Editor: Jai Seaman
Editorial assistant: Lauren Jacobs
Production editor: Ian Antcliff
Marketing manager: Catherine Slinn
Cover design: Shaun Mercier
Typeset by: C&M Digitals (P) Ltd, Chennai, India
Printed in the UK

Library of Congress Control Number: 2020940941

British Library Cataloguing in Publication data

A catalogue record for this book is available from
the British Library

ISBN 978-1-5297-4270-1

At SAGE we take sustainability seriously. Most of our products are printed in the UK using responsibly
sourced papers and boards. When we print overseas we ensure sustainable papers are used as measured
by the PREPS grading system. We undertake an annual audit to monitor our sustainability.

Contents

Everything in this book!

Section 1   How can I overcome writing anxiety?

Don't be beaten by writing anxiety. Recognise, reduce, and then resolve
your problems. Memories and experiences can make us anxious about
writing, but acknowledging them is the first step in beating them.

Section 2   How can I overcome writer's block?

Be aware of the causes, including tiredness, imposter syndrome,
perfectionism and not knowing where to start. Incorporate strategies to
start dealing with writer's block. Learn from the professionals.

Section 3   How can research help?

Researching a topic will give you a focused start on your work. It will
help when you are struggling for an idea or can't decide where to start.
Use note cards when researching.

Section 4   How can clustering and mind-mapping help?

Clustering helps a writer to summarise the ideas that they already have on a topic that they need to write about. Mind-mapping helps the writer to develop these ideas based on their new research.

Section 5   How can planning techniques help you to write?

Use the note card system to help you to plan your writing. After a process of selection and reorganisation you will have a structure and a plan for your piece of writing.

Section 6   How can keeping a journal help you to write?

Writing in a journal helps you to become a more perceptive, critical and reflective writer. Using a reflective model will help you to become a more self-reflective student too.

Section 7   How can freewriting help?

Freewriting will allow you to write without restrictions, anxiety or blocks. It also helps us to develop our thoughts about a topic.

Section 8   How can time management help you to write?

Creating a writing schedule, and keeping to it, will help you to feel less anxious about writing and in more control of your writing process. It will also help you to be more focused and productive.

How can I overcome writing anxiety?

10 second
summary

Memories and experiences can make us
anxious about writing, but acknowledging
them is the first step in beating them.

60 second summary

You can beat writing anxiety!

Many of us experience writing anxiety. From students to experienced and professional writers, writing anxiety can cause us to struggle with producing the text that we need. The good news is that there are techniques that we can use to overcome the problem of writing anxiety.

When we start a new project or course, we are often reminded of our previous struggles with writing. Memories of writing at school can often cause us to struggle with writing today. However, we can leave these memories and struggles in the past by focusing on the future.

You might think writers are special, but the best writers acknowledge that they are human and that they, too, struggle with writing sometimes. Reading about writers overcoming their difficulties can help you to overcome yours. Writing a list of specific difficulties, and acknowledging how they make you feel is the first step in beating your writing anxiety.

You are not alone

The first thing to realise is that many people suffer anxiety about writing. It can range from finding excuses to delay writing, to deliberately avoiding writing for long stretches of time. I've been writing for over 20 years, and I STILL experience both of these problems! Never fear, though, because there are ways we can overcome writing anxiety together. This is also true of writer's block, which we will talk more about in the next section.

Anxiety A feeling of nervousness or unease about something, or concerning something that needs to be done. Writing anxiety specifically relates to feelings of anxiety about writing, which often manifest themselves in avoidance of writing, procrastination and lack of confidence about your written work.

To some extent, all student and professional writers suffer from anxiety about writing. The key is to develop techniques and strategies to help you overcome the anxiety, and to kick start your writing. This is where you will find this book really useful.

Our experience of writing anxiety is often rooted in our relationships with writing throughout our lives. Many students begin a course with little recent experience of writing beyond their time in school or perhaps a college course. For some students, it may be many years since they were last in education and had to write a substantial piece of work.

As such, fear of failing is an entirely natural reaction to something that we haven't done for some time, and that includes writing. This can be made worse by having to write in a new context, such as beginning a course at university. But don't worry! This guide is here to help you overcome your fears.

Why do I feel anxious about writing?

You may be thinking about your previous experiences when you are trying to start writing. You may be thinking about bad memories of school, such as poor spelling test results. You might be remembering criticisms about your work that you received from teachers. Try to think of five past experiences about writing and note your feelings. If you can think of positive ones, as well as negative ones, then add those too!

Memories of writing anxiety

Complete the table below. (There is an example for you to refer to.)

Writing experiences	Feelings
When my high school English teacher told me that the paragraph I'd written in class 'didn't make sense'.	*I felt really embarrassed as my friends heard the comment and laughed.*
1	
2	
3	
4	
5	

Bad experiences can really knock your confidence, but you have to free yourself from the past and focus on the future. Beating anxiety about writing starts with identifying your own specific anxieties in the present time. By giving them a distinct written form you begin to grind down the vague, overwhelming sense of anxiety into a more distinct and manageable form. It gives you something more tangible to recognise and begin to deal with through using the advice in this book.

When you talk to other students, you might feel inadequate if some tell you how easy they find writing. However, it's important that you don't pay this too much attention. Simply nod and smile, and remember that they are not in a position to judge the success of their approach objectively. Most importantly, don't compare yourself to other students. Instead, focus your attention on your development as a writer.

It can be reassuring to read about how professional writers undertake the craft of writing, particularly those who are honest about their process. They often reveal the difficulties and anxieties involved in putting pen to paper, or fingers to keyboard. This should reassure us that our own anxieties are normal and that they can be overcome.

Reading about how professional writers approach their craft, and how they deal with anxieties, also demystifies the image many of us have of 'the writer' as being a gifted or special person. This creates a false standard that we feel we can never attain. The best writers are honest about this perception – it is complete nonsense. Writing may involve some talent, or skill, but much more can be learned through continued practice and developing the skills that you need.

DIY Current writing anxieties

What anxieties do you currently have about writing? Complete the table below. (There is an example for you to refer to.)

Anxiety levels:

  1 / 3 = low anxiety

  2 / 3 = medium anxiety

  3 / 3 = high anxiety

Current writing anxiety	Feelings	Anxiety level / 3
Starting the first draft of my next assignment.	*I'm struggling with the idea of sitting down at the laptop to start writing. I keep checking my email instead.*	*2 / 3*
1		
2		
3		
4		
5		

Now that you have written down your anxieties, you can start to look at them more objectively. Begin to think of them as problems to be solved, or even misconceptions that you can reject, rather than all-consuming, oppressive feelings. The good news is that the techniques in this book are designed to help you overcome *all* manner of problems with writing anxiety. Writing them down and giving them form on paper is the first step towards overcoming them.

Well done! You have taken the first step in beating your writing anxiety.

'Know your enemy! Learning about your own writing anxieties is the first step in beating them.'

CHECK POINT First steps in beating writing anxiety

You have started to think about the reasons for writing anxiety by looking at your feelings about writing in the past and in the present.

Check whether the following statements are true or false:

1   I now understand what writing anxiety is.......................................T/F

2   I can remember experiencing writing anxiety in the past............T/F

3   I have experienced writing anxiety recently...............................T/F

4   I recognise that writing anxiety is a problem that
    has solutions..T/F

A student told us

'I thought that only new students got anxious about their writing. Now I know that my lecturers and professional writers get anxious too, I feel better about it.'

How can I overcome writer's block?

10 second summary

Be aware of the causes and incorporate strategies to start dealing with writer's block.

Beginning to beat writer's block!

There are a number of causes of writer's block. These include tiredness, imposter syndrome, perfectionism and not knowing where to start with writing a piece of work. There are many professional and famous writers who have suffered, and suffer, writer's block and finding out more about this will help us to understand that this is a common problem among all kinds of writers. Useful strategies to try include walking, finding somewhere specific to write, and writing in a different location. Looking at how other writers have overcome writers block will also provide ideas for ways to beat it.

How can I overcome writer's block?

Writer's block occurs when your ability to write has stopped. It isn't related to a lack of commitment to a project, or negligence to undertake a writing-related task. It simply means that, for whatever reason, your ability to write is hindered.

There is no average length of time for experiencing writer's block. It can be temporary and ease in a short period of time, or it can affect a writer over a longer time period.

A student told us

'I just can't seem to make any progress with my work! I don't think I'll ever be able to write a university assignment that's good enough!'

Recent experiences with writer's block

In the table below, make a note of some of your recent experiences with writer's block. (There is an example for you to refer to.)

Writing experiences	Feelings
Starting my first assignment at uni.	*I felt really anxious and couldn't decide how to start my first draft. Should I write an Introduction? Start with the main body? I really struggled until I asked for some advice.*
1	
2	
3	
4	
5	

Listing your experiences will help you to recognise the signs should you encounter them again. Once you have identified these specific moments, you can start to think about how to overcome them.

Causes of writer's block

There are many possible causes of writer's block. Writing anxiety may play a part (see Section 1). Other factors include the following reasons.

Tiredness

Not feeling refreshed can hinder your ability to write.

When we are tired, our ability to think clearly is compromised. In order to overcome this, and for many other health reasons too, we need to maintain our physical and mental health. We need to establish good sleeping patterns. We need to balance our work, home, social and study commitments (see Section 8 for more help on time management).

Imposter syndrome

You may feel that you are not capable.

When you begin at university, everything might feel new, strange, scary and exciting. There are new people to meet, including lecturers, students, professional staff, operations staff and more. There is a whole new language to learn: for example, semester, tutorial, cohort, pedagogy. It takes time to become used to a new environment.

On top of this, when you start to receive your first assignments, you might experience new pangs of anxiety; many of us lack confidence and feel that we will struggle to complete the work. This is often when imposter syndrome kicks in. Imposter syndrome is where we doubt our achievements and feel like we are in danger of being a fraud. It often happens a short while after a new stage in our experience begins, such as beginning an undergraduate or postgraduate course of study.

Perfectionism

You may have unrealistically high standards and your 'inner critic' may question everything that you write. Perfectionism is the enemy of getting writing done. The pressure to produce good writing can hamper our ability to write, or even our ability to *start* writing.

This pressure of perfectionism is self-inflicted. We usually have an ideal image of our work as a completed thing in our mind. This is usually because our experience of other people's work is the final version in its final form. It's vital that we learn to lower our expectations at the starting point: writers do not create fully formed work at their very first attempt.

Not knowing where to start

You may feel overwhelmed by the scale of the writing project, which causes you to struggle with starting it.

How do I get over my writer's block?

There are a number of things that you can do to help begin to solve the problem of writer's block. Here are some suggestions.

Walking

Leaving your desk or workspace and going outside for a walk may seem like an unnecessary distraction, particularly if you need to get work done. However, if you are struggling with writer's block a walk can actually help you to deal with the problem. In a sense, by switching off from dealing with the immediate problem consciously, the distraction of being out in the world can enable your subconscious mind to get to work on the problem that you have.

Often, you will find that you have an idea that will help you to make some progress with your work when you least expect it. Be prepared for these instances! A pocket notebook is invaluable for recording these ideas while you are out and about. Similarly, a notes feature or voice recorder on a phone is also useful. But make sure that your device is fully charged before you leave home!

Find somewhere to write

It can help to treat writing like a part-time job. To do this, select a period of time and a place to work and try to minimise distractions. You can read more about time management in Section 8.

Try a different location

Take your notebook, or a laptop, and try writing in a different location. A change of scenery often helps to inspire new thoughts and ideas.

Keep moving

The secret is to keep moving with your writing, even if it is only to write about your feelings of frustration at your inability to write. Write anything to kick-start your writing muscles! Don't avoid writing, as you will become used to putting it off.

Also, don't wait until you feel like you want to write. Don't wait for ideas or inspiration to occur. The best way to make progress with your writing is simply to sit down and start to write. Write anything! Eventually, your brain will lead you to develop thoughts and ideas that may be useful later.

DIY How do other writer's deal with writer's block?

Search the internet for five pieces of advice from writers about overcoming writer's block.

Writer	Advice for overcoming writer's block
1	
2	
3	
4	
5	

Learning about how other writers have experienced writer's block, and how they have overcome it, shows us that we are not alone and that we can beat it too!

'Writer's blocks can be unblocked! You can beat it!'

CHECK POINT — Recognise your writer's block

You have started to think about the reasons for writer's block by looking at its causes. Now respond to the following prompts:

I now understand what writer's block is .... T/F

I have identified potential causes of my writer's block. These are:

1 ....

2 ....

3 ....

How can research
help?

*10 second
summary*

When we are struggling for an idea or
can't decide where to start, researching
a topic can help give us a focused start.

60 second
summary

Finders keepers! Researching to write

Knowing where and how to begin a piece of writing can be really difficult, and anxiety inducing. Researching a topic helps us to find a way of starting a writing project in a disciplined and effective way by helping us to identify and explore an aspect of a topic in a methodical manner.

Rather than searching aimlessly for resources, it is useful to ask a librarian to help you get started. Using the SERENE method will ensure that you search for, and find, resources that are relevant to the piece of writing or academic assignment that you need to complete.

How can research help?

One of the main difficulties when we experience writer's block and writing anxiety is that we do not have any idea of what to write about, or even where to start writing. We may experience a total blank or, conversely, be overloaded with so many things to consider that we feel like we are drowning in possibilities!

Research A systematic investigation to establish facts and inform conclusions. When writing, knowledge is power, and the more information and facts we have about a topic before we write, the more prepared we will be to write a successful piece.

One significant and helpful way to overcome this problem is to undertake research in a measured and methodical way. This will allow you to begin thinking about specific aspects of a topic, for those of you who are experiencing a mental blank.

Alternatively, for those of you who are overwhelmed by many potential avenues, you will be able to begin a focused exploration of a single path.

The SERENE method

In order to begin to research successfully, and move towards beating your writer's block and anxiety, you can adopt the SERENE method. The word serene means peaceful, calm and untroubled, and that is certainly the state of mind we are aiming for when we are writing! The stages of SERENE are as follows:

S   Search

E   Evaluate

R   Read

E   Examine

N   Note-making

E   Evaluate your progress

We will now look at each stage in turn.

Search

Appointment with a librarian

The best librarians won't do your searching for you; they will show you the skills and techniques that you need to use in order to make the best use of library catalogues, online resources and databases. They will help you to develop an effective approach to searching these resources. Here are some approaches that librarians suggest you adopt.

Library catalogues and databases

Your university will have a library catalogue and a range of databases that are accessible electronically. You should find that there are terminals housed in the library building. In addition, catalogues and databases can be accessed via the internet, so you can search for items wherever you have an internet connection! I am old enough to remember index cards in boxes, so I see the advantages of the online connectivity of library catalogues for research and writing!

Search strategies

Boolean searching is an effective way of finding relevant resources. Select words and phrases (search terms) that are relevant to your topic. In addition, use the following terms to further define and refine your search:

AND

OR

NOT

AND will search for all of the terms that it connects;

OR will search for any of the terms that it connects, but not necessarily both;

NOT will not search for any of the terms used after it.

So, a search for the following:

Fish AND Chips

Would bring up results containing both terms.

A search for:

Fish OR Chips

Would bring up results containing either term.

A search for:

Fish NOT chips

Would only bring up results featuring the term Fish.

Evaluate

As you look through your search results, and before you make a commitment to reading a text in its entirety, it will prove useful to undertake a preliminary evaluation of it. To do this, assess the following points.

Currency

When was the article, book etc. published? Is it considered current within your subject or field of study? This is vitality important. For medical subjects, research and publications need to have been published recently, as research findings influence changes in this area. However, for subjects such as English Literature, research and literary criticism published decades ago can still be valid and useful to use.

Quality

Judge the quality of the source that you are thinking of using. Consider the publisher – are they reputable? Consider the url – a gov.uk indicates a government website, while an ac.uk indicates an educational website; both would be considered reputable sources.

Peer-reviewed (academic)

Publication in peer-reviewed journals is an indicator of quality. 'Peer review' means that the publication has been reviewed by a selection of the author's peers, and revised by the author according to their suggestions. This serves to strengthen the accuracy and validity of a publication.

Keywords

Individual search results will often be accompanied by a list of relevant keywords. Looking at these will help you to judge whether or not a resource may potentially be useful or not.

Abstracts

An abstract is a short summary, usually a detailed paragraph, which contains the main points of the article or text it relates to. Reading an abstract can help you to judge whether or not it is worth your time to read the entire text.

Read

It can be tempting to read through your articles and chapters speedily, switching between multiple sources to try and find potentially useful information and ideas. However, flitting between pieces can often make us feel overwhelmed. Make a conscious decision to select and read one piece of work at a time in order to maintain focus.

Examine

While you are reading, bear in mind what you want to know and need to know to fulfil the piece of writing that you are doing. This will help you to select relevant information and ideas and not move away on a tangent from the requirements of your assignment.

Note-making

Make your own notes while you are reading. If you can, make your notes using a pen and paper, and write them on note or index cards. Note cards should contain one note per card, and allow for easier planning later (see Section 5).

Note cards these are rectangular-shaped pieces of card, lined or unlined, that can be written on. Standard sizes are 5 x 3" or 6 x 4". They are also known as index cards. They are useful in the research and planning stages of writing.

Evaluate your progress

Once you have completed notes on the sources that you selected, read through your notes. Ask yourself whether or not you feel that you have enough to start writing. If not, don't worry! It's completely normal at this stage. Remember that research is an iterative process, meaning that it has to be repeated in order to ensure depth and rigour.

A student told us

'Using the SERENE method really helped me to search for resources that were actually relevant to my assignment, and not ones that turned out to be of no help.'

'Research is the fuel for our writing engine!'

CHECK POINT Using SERENE

Make sure that you followed all of the stages of SERENE when you were looking for resources for your latest assignment.

Tick off the following when you have done them:

Search ☐

Evaluate ☐

Read ☐

Examine ☐

Note-making ☐

Evaluate your progress ☐

How can clustering and mind-mapping help?

10 second summary

Clustering can help you summarise your existing ideas on the topic you will write about. Mind-mapping will help you to develop your ideas following your research.

**Feeling flustered? Use some clusters! Research mishap?
Use mind-maps!**

Clustering helps us to organise our existing ideas on topics that we are
going to write about. Using a series of bubbles, connected together with
lines, we can get our ideas down on paper, in order to gain an overview
of them. This will help us to begin to think about aspects of a topic that
we can then begin to research and look into more deeply.

Mind-mapping helps us to add new knowledge to our clusters, which we
gain through new research and reading. We can identify new ideas and
form connections between ideas and concepts by forming connections
between bubbles. We can add to, edit and delete bubbles from clusters
and add new ones to form mind-maps that will help us in our aim to write
successfully.

How can clustering and mind-mapping help?

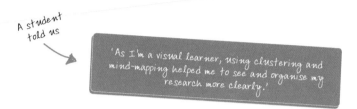

'As I'm a visual learner, using clustering and mind-mapping helped me to see and organise my research more clearly.'

Clustering and mind-mapping are often seen as being the same process but with different names. However, it is useful for us to make a distinction between them in terms of their use.

Clustering can be used before you search for and read through resources. Mind-mapping should be used after you have found and read resources on your topic.

Mind-mapping A way of recording the new knowledge that you have gained from your research and reconfiguring it in new connections and relationships. It also builds upon the clusters you formed before your research.

Clustering

Clustering is a technique that enables you to identify and record your existing knowledge on a topic. It is helpful to do this because it establishes a starting point for your level of knowledge on a topic before you begin your additional research.

It is a visual process in which you create shapes or bubbles containing content that you can link together. For example, the centre shape often contains the topic, or a sub-topic, of your research.

Let's look at an example based on the assignment title *Evaluate the impact of British creators on the American comic book industry in the 1980s*. We could start with a central bubble like this:

Additional shapes or bubbles can branch out as you break down and develop aspects within the topic:

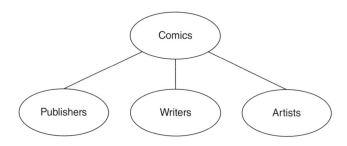

Here, three bubbles have been added – publishers, writers and artists.

Further bubbles containing content linked to these aspects can then be added:

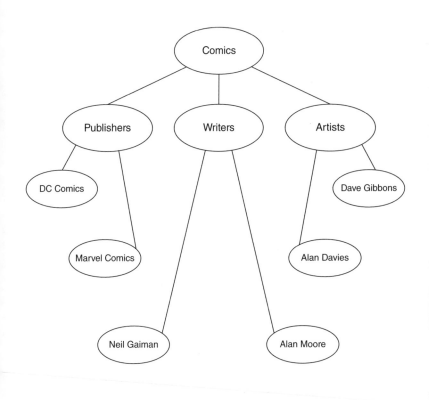

Here, two publishers, two writers and two artists have been added.

Links between bubbles can also be identified:

Here, we see that Alan Moore is linked to Neil Gaiman; Moore taught Gaiman how to correctly structure a script for a comic book.

Do not overthink when creating your clusters. You do not have to limit, censor or edit at this stage. Put down everything that you can remember about the aspect of the topic you will be writing about. Use clustering as a way of splurging content onto paper. Using pen and paper is a really easy way of doing this, although you can use a relevant software package too. You can edit later, once you are sure that you have explored all of your options.

Clustering A way of representing your existing knowledge on a topic in a series of linked balloons. Clustering is most useful when it is done before new research, as a way of consolidating your existing knowledge on a topic.

DIY — Let's cluster!

Choose a subject and create a cluster using the blank cluster here:

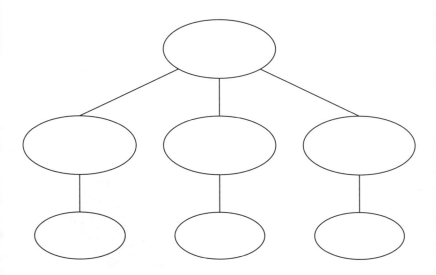

You have now identified some of your own initial thoughts on the topic that you have selected.

Mind-mapping

For mind-mapping, you can take selected sections of your cluster and add, prune and extend them with the extra knowledge that you gained from your research. This is where you can begin to identify how these new ideas, facts and pieces of knowledge can form related concepts, comment on each other, and seem to fit together. This will help you with the planning stage of writing, which is covered in Section 5.

Please note that you will find your initial clusters will change as you incorporate the ideas and knowledge that you have gained in your research. Don't be alarmed if some of your initial clusters are no longer relevant and need to be deleted. This is a normal part of the evolution of your research.

Using the cluster I created earlier for the comics assignment, I undertook research to develop and deepen my knowledge on the topic. I can now take a cluster and extend it into a mind-map, by adding my new research and knowledge.

For example, I discovered that Neil Gaiman's first work in America was for DC comics, with a series called *Black Orchid*. He then went on to publish the award-winning *Sandman* series with the same publisher. I can add these new facts from research to develop my mind-map:

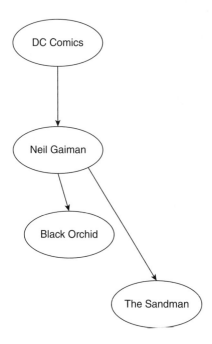

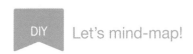

Using the cluster you created earlier, choose one aspect and find some additional information about it. Then extend that section of the cluster with a mind-map using the diagram here.

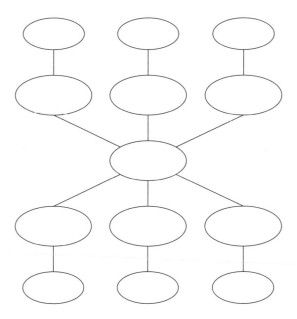

You have now begun to build on your pre-existing knowledge with new research, and begun to organise it with a mind-map.

'Map your way to writing success!'

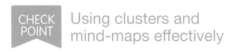
Follow this checklist to make sure that you have followed the process of creating a cluster and a mind-map effectively.

Cluster – before you begin research:

Started with a central cluster(s) topic (or more)　☐

Added relevant sub-topics　☐

Added sub-sub topics to each sub-topic　☐

Mind-map – after you have undertaken research:

Selected each central cluster and associated bubbles　☐

Added new information in new bubbles　☐

Deleted obsolete bubbles　☐

Congratulations!

You now have a comprehensive amount of research and ideas to use in planning your next piece of work.

How can planning techniques help you to write?

10 second
summary

Using note cards that you have created will help you to create a plan and a structure for your piece of writing. Planning makes for easier writing.

60 second summary

Good planning makes good writing!

You can gather all of the cards that you have written during the note-taking process and re-read them. As you are reading them, you will begin to identify common ideas, themes and features between certain cards, so group these cards together by these themes. This will give you a clearer idea of the aspects your work will cover.

Take each themed pile of cards and re-read them again. Put them in a new order that feels logical to you. Once you have done this, put your individual piles in an order that feels logical to you. At any stage of the process you can make changes. At the end you will have a writing plan!

How can planning techniques help you to write?

You are now ready to begin the process of developing the content you created when you were researching (see Section 3), clustering and mind-mapping (see Section 4). Refining, reorganising and developing your content into a coherent plan will make the actual process of writing a piece much easier to accomplish.

Note cards

A good place to start will be to gather together your notes. Using index or note cards, as advised in Section 3, will have stood you in good stead for this planning phase. Take your stack of cards and lay them out on a large surface, such as a table, kitchen counter, or even a floor. Read through each card and, as you identify a subject, concept or theme that some of the cards hold in common, group them together in separate piles. The decision is yours! You are in control of this selection process.

Don't worry too much about whether there is a right or wrong approach to this selection process because it is fluid and allows for flexibility and change. You may decide to switch cards, which is fine and a normal part of the planning process.

Once you have done this, review each group of cards.

Assess and select

You should review each group of cards and reorder them based on what you feel or perceive to be a logical order. Re-read the cards and consider your responses to the following questions:

Do you feel anything needs changing on an index card?

Can any cards be taken out of the group?

Should any cards be placed in another group?

Should any cards be filed to one side because they are no longer relevant?

It can be tempting to get rid of cards that you feel you no longer need during this process. Don't throw away these cards. Later on, you may find that you need them after all. Alternatively, you may discover that they are useful for a future writing project. Nothing is ever wasted by the writer!

Organising your card groups

Once you have settled on the order of cards within each group, you can then decide on an overall order of the main groups of cards themselves, i.e. the group of cards on *this* topic go first, followed by this *other* topic, etc.

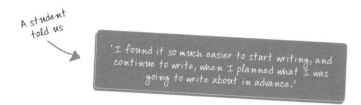

A student told us

'I found it so much easier to start writing, and continue to write, when I planned what I was going to write about in advance.'

Create linking cards

In addition to the notes you have taken from sources, which you will have reordered into groups, and sub-ordered within each group.

You will need to discuss your interpretation of them. You will also need to construct an argument, make valid points, and the other associated elements of writing that make up an academic piece of work beyond the evidence and ideas of others that you have found.

Linking cards These contain a point, comment, interpretation etc. made by the writer, created as a part of the planning process for writing. These can be used at the planning stage to create a plan for your writing.

In order to do this, you can create some linking cards. Each card will contain a summary of one of your own points, comments, interpretations, etc. These can be interwoven with the existing packs of cards you have written notes on from your resources.

This will then enable you to create a planned structure, or order, to follow in order to write a draft of your work. You may find that you end up changing card order or group order to facilitate the new points that you are adding. This is fine, and is a normal part of the planning process. You are aiming to write the most well planned and structured piece of writing that you can, so changes show that you are taking due care to do this.

Structure The logical and planned organisation of material in a piece of writing. The three main elements of the structure of a standard piece of academic writing, such as the essay, are the introduction, main body, and conclusion.

Structure

The standard three part structure of an academic piece of writing contains an **introduction**, **main body** and **conclusion**. It is good advice to focus on the main body first; it is easier to write an introduction and a conclusion for a piece of work that already exists.

You can now use the stacks of cards, precisely ordered to your needs, as a route map to write your main body. Each card will be the springboard to a short piece of text – sentence, quotation, paraphrase, paragraph – that you will write up more fully.

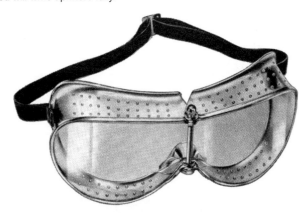

Planning makes perfect!

Make sure you have taken each of the following steps in the order below.

Re-read your note cards ☐

Grouped cards by theme ☐

Reordered each card in a group logically ☐

Reorganised the order of the groups ☐

Written and added linking cards ☐

Finalised the entire order ☐

'Move forward with your writing, having the confidence to know what you are going to write about in advance!'

Congratulations!

You have planned your piece of writing!

How can keeping a journal help you to write?

10 second
summary

Using a journal helps you to become a more perceptive and reflective writer.

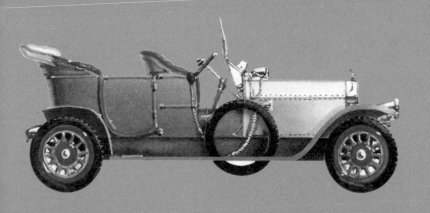

A journal is your passport to success!

We are often focused on producing writing for assessment as a student, but writing can be used to develop and improve our critical thinking and self-reflection skills. Writing a journal regularly helps us to become a better writer, thinker and student.

Using a new way to write helps us to approach journal writing in a different way from writing for assessment. For example, PC users can try writing by hand, which can be a refreshing way to approach journal writing.

You can think about your encounters with new knowledge and begin to question, assess and evaluate new ideas and concepts in your journal without the restrictions of assignment writing. You will then continue to develop as a writer and a reader. You can also use a reflective model in your journal writing to assess and analyse your own experiences more deeply and systematically.

How can keeping a journal help you to write?

It is easy to become caught up in the hectic whirlwind of being a student. It can often be a busy period in your life, one in which you experience many new things. You will also learn about many new ideas, concepts, theories and more.

At university, much of our learning is driven towards assessment. We generally finish modules with some form of written assessment such as an assignment, report or exam. Due to this need, it is inevitable that we are focused primarily on the production of writing that is assessed. That's natural, and important, and you need to ensure that you keep writing with this in mind.

However, there is more to learning, and writing, than just the production of assignments, reports, exams and other assessments. Lecturers are keen for students to develop critical thinking and self-reflection skills. In addition, these are also prized skills in life beyond university. While there are opportunities to show evidence of both skills at university, these are naturally limited by the occasional nature of assessments; we spend a few weeks preparing for a specific piece of work before final submission, and then it's effectively over, bar receiving our grade and feedback.

However, the more critical thinking and self-reflection that you do through your writing, the more effective a writer and thinker you can become. Keeping a journal is a surefire way to becoming a better writer and thinker! The more you do something, the better you become at doing it. Writing a daily journal will help you to improve your writing, critical thinking and self-reflection skills, which will ultimately make you a more successful student and writer!

Journal A record of your thoughts, opinions, ideas, reflections and more, written on a regular basis. It can be written by hand or typed, as per the preference of each writer and student. Using a journal will help you to improve as a learner and a writer.

A student told us

'Writing a journal has helped me to become a more perceptive and analytical writer and student.'

Your writing journal

There is no one specific way to start a writing journal. However, there are a number of common variants, which are:

- A bound notebook;

- Loose leaf pages, kept in a binder;

- A Word document or similar;

It is often a good idea to use one of the above that you would not normally use for writing. For example, if your usual work involves using a PC during the day (like me), it can be refreshing to use a bound notebook for your journal writing. It will be easier to disassociate this particular kind of reflective writing from your usual written work.

Thinking about your learning

Journal writing will to help you to develop an ongoing, deeper engagement with your topics, rather than just for the limited purposes of assignment writing. However, parts of your journal writing may feed into your other written work too.

Here are some things to consider writing about in your journal:

- Questions you have about a topic you've read about or covered in a lecture;
- Ideas you have for writing projects;
- Your responses to ideas, perspectives or concepts that you encounter.

Use your journal as a way of talking to yourself, by asking the questions you have about a subject and noting down ways that you could start to answer or address these. Write about your reactions to ideas you encounter during your reading, in your lecture, or in a seminar. Treat your journal as a deep discussion with yourself.

1   Try to use a writing method that you would not normally use, for instance a notepad if you normally type.

2   Write a journal entry and date it with today's date. Choose a topic that you have found particularly interesting and ask yourself what, specifically, you found interesting about it.

3   Record your personal thoughts and feelings about it. That way, you can develop an interest in your topic, and even a passion for it!

Using a reflective writing model

You can also use your journal to reflect on your thoughts and experiences in a more systematic way. To do this, there are a number of different reflective writing models that you can use in your journal writing, should you wish to do so. These are useful for those times when you feel you need to assess or examine a particular experience in a more structured way.

There are many different kinds of reflective models that you can use. My particular favourite is the model created by Gary Rolfe and his colleagues. It is clear and useful. It is based on three questions that are designed to elicit reflection. These are:

Reflective model A method used to create a structured and considered response to specific past experiences. Various models exist, such as Rolfe's model (used in this book).

Rolfe's model of reflection A model of reflection, created by Gary Rolfe and his colleagues, which utilises three stages: What?; So what?; and Now what?

What?	What happened? Describe your experience.
So what?	So what was significant about the experience?
Now what?	Now what can / could be done the same, or differently, next time?

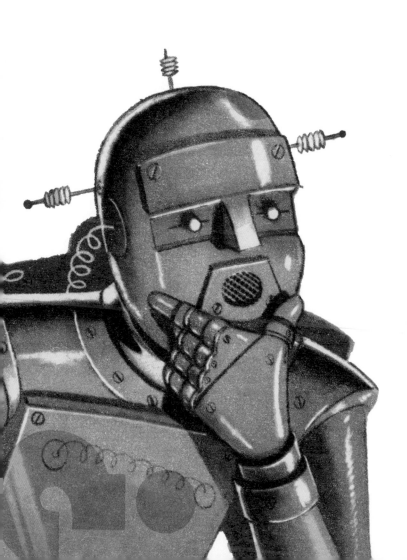

Rolfe's model of reflection

Choose a recent event and apply Rolfe's model of reflection to it.

What?

_____

_____

_____

So what?

_____

_____

_____

_____

_____

_____

_____

Now what?

Using this method, you have now begun to write reflectively and think more deeply and critically about your experience.

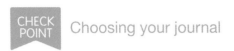

CHECK POINT Choosing your journal

Choose the type of a journal you will use:

Notebook ☐

Loose paper and binder ☐

PC or laptop ☐

Other ☐

Have you:

Completed your first journal entry? .... Yes/No

Used a reflective model in your journal writing? .... Yes/No

If you have answered No to either of these questions, re-read Section 6, before answering again.

> 'Your journal is your way to become a better writer!'

How can freewriting help?

10 second summary

Freewriting allows us to write without restrictions, anxiety or blocks. It helps us to feel easier about writing. It helps us to develop our thoughts about a topic too.

Writing without pressure!

Throughout the drafting stage, we often feel the pressure of producing the final piece of writing. We are conscious that our work has to be read by other people. This pressure can cause writing anxiety and writer's blocks.

Freewriting and looping is a technique that encourages us to write for ourselves. We can think and write for only ourselves. Writing in this way helps us to develop our writing muscles too. It helps us to feel more comfortable and at ease with the writing process.

How can freewriting help?

Writing to be read

When we are writing, we are generally focused on the end product – producing a well-crafted, grammatically correct, purpose-driven piece of work. We often feel what I like to call the *pressure of the final piece*.

It often means that we can be too critical of what we are writing throughout the whole writing process. Our 'inner editor' seems to constantly encourage us to delete, amend and tweak our writing after every phrase and sentence.

This can be exhausting, and lead to an increase in our writing anxiety. It can lead to writer's block too, as we lose faith in our work when we compare it to previously published examples.

Writing not to be read

To overcome this, we need to adopt a process that involves writing for yourself,

Inner editor When we are overly critical of our initial writing efforts, to a detrimental degree. The inner editor is a negative manifestation of our doubts when we begin to write the first draft of a piece of work, and should be ignored. Editing should always be separated from writing, and occur after a writing session (preferably after as long a break as possible).

Freewriting Writing without conscious restrictions and attention to conventional rules and expectation. Using writing for practise and to develop thoughts and ideas. Writing for ourselves, not an audience. Freewriting is writing without limitations. Spelling, punctuation and grammar can be ignored in freewriting, as expression is of more importance at this stage.

or writing *not* to be read. This is the essence of freewriting and looping, which both enables us to be practise the skills and process of writing in itself, in addition to accessing some of our unconscious thoughts. It is the antithesis of writing to be read, in that you do not need to focus on grammar, spelling, punctuation or even making complete sense. In fact, perhaps for the first time in your life, write with no filters or restrictions.

The only rule is that you write about an aspect of the assignment or topic that you need to cover for an assessment. But don't write for the actual assignment. Loosen your writing muscles and have fun!

Looping Used during the freewriting process, looping is the selection of one element of a piece of freewriting and writing more about it in the next piece of freewriting. It is a process of extension and refinement and allows our initial thoughts to develop more fully and extensively.

Freewriting and looping are surefire ways of easing writing anxiety and beating writer's block!

Looping

Begin your freewriting exercise by choosing a specific topic that you have been writing about. Then set a timer for a short period of time – no more than five or ten minutes. Then begin writing, and start with anything at all.

Here is an important point to remember: continue writing even if you can't think what to write! If this is the case, simply write something like 'I don't know what to write right now.' Write about how you feel about a topic, use the first person, use slang and corrections and misspellings – all of the things that you can't do in academic writing. Do not go back and edit this piece of freewriting for content either.

At the end of your five-or ten-minute period, finish the sentence you are writing. Take a short break. Then return to your piece of work and select one idea or element that strikes you as interesting. Using this as a focus or prompt, begin a second period of freewriting. This looping technique can be repeated a few times in order to generate thoughts and ideas, and to develop your writing muscles.

A student told us

'Freewriting is so liberating! I feel more comfortable writing than I did before, and much less anxious. I now realise that I can experiment with and alter anything I write, including drafts for uni!'

DIY   Freewriting and looping

Let's do some freewriting and looping.

1   Think about your next assignment or piece of writing. Choose one aspect of it.

2   Write without stopping or editing for five or ten minutes.

3   Take a short break.

4   Re-read your work. Choose one element that you could write more about.

5   Write on this element for five or ten minutes.

6   Read and repeat the process as required.

Benefits of freewriting

Freewriting and looping makes us more used to expressing ourselves in writing more naturally and more regularly, rather than during the more limited time of assignment production. It creates more comfort and ease with the writing process itself.

It can also help us to generate new ideas and new angles on a topic to write about. Here, freewriting is an aid to thinking about the specific topic at hand. Rather than musing unconsciously about something, we are taking a more proactive approach to thinking and developing our ideas.

Develop your freewriting

Allocate time in your schedule to freewrite regularly – ideally on a daily basis.

Try the process for at least a week.

This will help you to practise your writing regularly. It helps you to maintain a regular writing schedule too. Freewriting is also an excellent exercise to use to warm up your writing muscles.

Regular freewriting periods will help you to feel more comfortable with the writing process and avoid writing anxiety and writer's block.

'Freewriting set my writing free!'

CHECK POINT Get freewriting right

Are you following the freewriting stages fully, in the following order?

1	Choose an element / aspect of a topic	Yes / No
2	Freewrite for five or ten minutes	Yes / No
3	Do not edit as you write	Yes / No
4	Take a short break	Yes / No
5	Re-read your work	Yes / No
6	Choose one aspect	Yes / No
7	Freewrite about it for five to ten minutes	Yes / No
8	Repeat as needed	Yes / No

If you have answered No to any of the above, re-read this section and try again.

How can time management help you to write?

10 second
summary

Deciding when to write, and sticking to a schedule, will help you to feel less anxious about the writing process.

60 second summary

Make time work for you!

Being proactive and deciding when to write will lessen anxiety about the writing process. We should plan our writing schedule in advance. For writing at university, we need to think about our time in three distinct, but interlinked, ways – over the next academic year, each week, and each day.

We can use an academic calendar to plan the year ahead. We can use weekly planners to designate specific periods of time for our writing. We can use the Pomodoro Technique to write, stay refreshed and maintain our focus.

How can time management help you write?

Time travel

Many of us would love to experience time travel. Our desire is particularly strong when we have a deadline fast approaching! We wish that we had made better use of our time, not been so distracted, or started earlier. This can increase our writing anxiety as well as lead us to develop writing blocks through panicking. We no doubt regret that we don't have the ability to time travel!

However, we *are* time travelers, in our own way. It's just that we are limited to travelling into the future at the rate of one second at a time, one minute, one hour, one day and so on. There is good news though. Rather than be locked in by time, we can be proactive and use our time to our advantage, by adopting the following time management process.

Three-part process

This process involves you organising your time in three different, but interlinked, ways: by year, by week, and by day.

Planning your year

At the start of each term students receive a vast amount of information. Among this, they will see details of assignment deadlines, assessments and other related events. This information may well be distributed between different documents, such as multiple course handbooks. It is useful to gather these dates together in one easily accessible place, in order for it to be transferred to an academic calendar.

An academic calendar, unlike a normal calendar, generally runs from September to the following August. This reflects the standard period of time when students are on campus, as well as writing and submitting their academic work. Begin by entering the deadlines for your work on an academic calendar. These can be found online quite easily: www.calendarpedia.co.uk contains many useful ones, which are free to download.

You can then begin to block out days and weeks to devote to specific assignments and tasks. Be realistic with the time that you have available. Count back the weeks from your deadline to now. Allocate your weeks appropriately, considering whether it is better for you to focus on one writing task over a week or more before moving on to the next, or whether you feel you prefer to multi-task within any specific shorter period of time.

Planning your week

Even when we are not writing, we are often thinking about writing. Sometimes we are anxious because we don't feel we have the time to actually get any writing done! We can be out and about, doing our daily chores, attending lectures, doing paid work, and more, and in the back of our minds we are telling ourselves:

'I need to start that assignment.'

'I haven't made much progress on the piece for the next seminar.'

'I don't know when I'll be able to start that essay!'

Stop thinking about not writing. Instead, spend some time planning when in the week you will devote yourself to your writing. Use a weekly planner to decide where in your schedule you can commit to write. That way, when you start to worry that you are not getting any writing done, you can reassure yourself that you have time later that day, or later in the week, that is your protected writing time. Negotiate with family and friends to ensure that they understand that your writing time is a commitment that should not normally be compromised.

Here is an example:

	Mon	Tues	Weds	Thurs	Fri	Sat	Sun
9.00 – 10.00		*Work*		*Work*			
10.00 – 11.00	*Lecture*	*Work*	*Lecture*	*Work*	*Lecture*		
11.00 – 12.00	*Lecture*	*Work*	*Lecture*	*Work*	*Lecture*		
12.00 – 13.00		*Work*		*Work*			
13.00 – 14.00	*Lecture*	*Work*	*Lecture*	*Work*		*Writing*	
14.00 – 15.00	*Lecture*	*Work*	*Lecture*	*Work*	*Lecture*	*Writing*	
15.00 – 16.00		*Work*		*Work*	*Lecture*	*Writing*	
16.00 – 17.00		*Work*		*Work*		*Writing*	
17.00 – 18.00							
18.00 – 19.00							
19.00 – 20.00	*Writing*	*Writing*		*Writing*	*Writing*		
20.00 – 21.00	*Writing*	*Writing*		*Writing*	*Writing*		
21.00 – 22.00							
22.00 – 23.00							

Plan your week

Using the weekly planner, plan your own week. Incorporate writing time and non-writing time (for lectures and other commitments).

	Mon	Tues	Weds	Thurs	Fri	Sat	Sun
9.00 – 10.00							
10.00 – 11.00							
11.00 – 12.00							
12.00 – 13.00							
13.00 – 14.00							
14.00 – 15.00							
15.00 – 16.00							
16.00 – 17.00							
17.00 – 18.00							
18.00 – 19.00							
19.00 – 20.00							
20.00 – 21.00							
21.00 – 22.00							
22.00 – 23.00							

Treat your writing like a part-time job and give it the time and respect that it deserves. This will help you to maintain a balance between all of the demands on your time.

Planning your day

The Pomodoro Technique was invented by Francesco Cirillo as an aid to focus and productivity. It is an incredibly useful technique to use when you are writing, and for all forms of study and work. In order to use this technique you will need a timer. Any timer will do; Cirillo used an oven timer shaped like a tomato, hence the name of the technique: pomodoro is the Italian word for tomato.

Pomodoro Technique
Created by Francesco Cirillo, the Pomodoro Technique is a time management method that helps you to stay focused and productive. It suggests using 25-minute work periods alternating with 5-minute rest periods. It can help you to ensure that you take regular breaks. It can also act as a prompt to beat procrastination.

The Pomodoro Technique

Follow these instructions:

1   Choose your writing task.
2   Set your timer for 25 minutes ('one pomodoro').
3   Write, without interruption, for 25 minutes.
4   After 25 minutes, take a timed 5-minute break.

Repeat this process as time allows in your weekly planner.

After four pomodoros, take a longer break, of at least 15 minutes. If your planning allows, begin another pomodoro work period and continue the process described above.

The Pomodoro Technique is helpful for people who work for hours on end, as it reminds them to take regular breaks in order to stay refreshed. It is also helpful for procrastinators, as they can use the technique to encourage themselves to complete a 25-minute period, after which they are more likely to continue working as time allows in their schedule.

A student told us

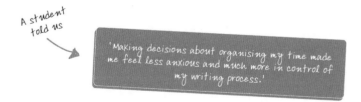

'Making decisions about organising my time made me feel less anxious and much more in control of my writing process.'

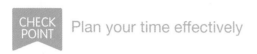

CHECK POINT Plan your time effectively

Make sure you have completed the following:

Obtained an academic year calendar ☐

Added your deadlines for the year ☐

Allocated weeks to your goals ☐

Completed a weekly planner for the week ahead ☐

Obtained a timer ☐

Used the Pomodoro Technique ☐

'Don't be controlled by time! You can control time instead!'

Congratulations!

You are now an effective manager of your writing time!

Final checklist: How to know you are done

To help ensure that you are fully prepared to beat your writer's block, work through this checklist.

Do you know why you get anxious about your writing?
If not, go back to Section 1. ☐

Do you know why you get writer's block? If not,
go back to Section 2. ☐

Have you have researched the topic that you
are going to write about? If not, go back to Section 3. ☐

Have you used clustering and mind-mapping techniques before you start writing? If not, go back to Section 4. ❏

Have you put together a plan for before you start writing? If not, go back to Section 5 ❏

Have you begun to keep a journal to help you become a better writer? If not, go back to Section 6. ❏

Are you using freewriting and looping to practise your writing? If not, go back to Section 7. ❏

Are you managing your time and have you created a writing schedule? If not, go back to Section 8. ❏

Glossary

Anxiety A feeling of nervousness or unease about something, or concerning something that needs to be done. Writing anxiety specifically relates to feelings of anxiety about writing, which often manifest themselves in avoidance of writing, procrastination and lack of confidence about your written work.

Boolean operators Using AND, OR, NOT to refine your searches. Using these terms helps you to create more focused searches on online databases:

> AND will search for all of the terms that it connects;
>
> OR will search for any of the terms that it connects (but not necessarily both);
>
> NOT won't search for the terms used after it.

Clustering A way of representing your existing knowledge on a topic in a series of linked balloons. Clustering is most useful when it is done before new research, as a way of consolidating your existing knowledge on a topic.

Freewriting Writing without conscious restrictions and attention to conventional rules and expectation. Using writing for practise and to develop thoughts and ideas. Writing for ourselves, not an audience. Freewriting is writing without limitations. Spelling, punctuation and grammar can be ignored in freewriting, as expression is of more importance at this stage.

Imposter syndrome When someone doubts their achievements and feels that they are not deserving of their status or role. In writing terms, this often relates to how we view writers as being special and a role that we cannot aspire to. This is an unhelpful misconception.

Inner editor When we are overly critical of our initial writing efforts, to a detrimental degree. The inner editor is a negative manifestation of our doubts when we begin to write the first draft of a piece of work, and should be ignored. Editing should always be separated from writing, and occur after a writing session (preferably after as long a break as possible).

Journal A record of your thoughts, opinions, ideas, reflections and more, written on a regular basis. It can be written by hand or typed, as per the preference of each writer and student. Using a journal will help you to improve as a learner and a writer.

Linking cards These contain a point, comment, interpretation etc. made by the writer, created as a part of the planning process for writing. These can be used at the planning stage to create a plan for your writing.

Looping Used during the freewriting process, looping is the selection of one element of a piece of freewriting and writing more about it in the next piece of freewriting. It is a process of extension and refinement and allows our initial thoughts to develop more fully and extensively.

Mind-mapping A way of recording the new knowledge that you have gained from your research and reconfiguring it in new connections and relationships. It also builds upon the clusters you formed before your research.

Note cards These are rectangular-shaped pieces of card, lined or unlined, that can be written on. Standard sizes are 5 x 3" or 6 x 4". They are also known as index cards. They are useful in the research and planning stages of writing.

Pomodoro Technique Created by Francesco Cirillo, the Pomodoro Technique is a time management method that helps you to stay focused and productive. It suggests using 25-minute work periods alternating with 5-minute rest periods. It can help you to ensure that you take regular breaks. It can also act as a prompt to beat procrastination.

Reflective model A method used to create a structured and considered response to specific past experiences. Various models exist, such as Rolfe's model (used in this book).

Research A systematic investigation to establish facts and inform conclusions. When writing, knowledge is power, and the more information and facts we have about a topic before we write, the more prepared we will be to write a successful piece.

Rolfe's model of reflection A model of reflection, created by Gary Rolfe and his colleagues, which utilises the following three stages:

What?	What happened? Describe your experience.
So what?	So what was significant about the experience?
Now what?	Now what can / could be done the same, or differently, next time?

Serene In normal usage, serene means peaceful, calm and untroubled. In relation to writing and research, it refers to the SERENE method, outlined in Section 3 of this book. SERENE is an acronym that stands for: Search – Evaluate – Read – Examine – Note-making – Evaluate your progress.

Structure The logical and planned organisation of material in a piece of writing. The three main elements of the structure of a standard piece of academic writing, such as the essay, are the introduction, main body, and conclusion.

Further reading

Polish Your Academic Writing by Helen Coleman is another Sage Super Quick Skills book that really helps students to focus on how to write a great piece of academic writing. This is highly recommended, as is *Your Super Quick Guide to University* by the same author.

Peter Elbow's work is really helpful in developing a democratic approach to writing. Elbow says that 'anyone can write', and I agree. Any of his books on writing are useful. A Google search for Peter Elbow AND writing is a good place to start learning more about his work.

William Zinnser's *On Writing Well* is a good guide for non-fiction writers, and a well-written and engaging book in itself too.

Stephen King's *On Writing*, despite focusing on fiction, emphasises the tools and temperament all writers need to succeed.